YOUR FIRST OR

Where and how to gro

Authors: John Blowers and

Publishers: The Eric Young Orchid Foundation

CONTENTS:

The Eric Young Orchid Foundation

Introduction

PART ONE **KNOW YOUR PLANTS**

Their Names: species and hybrids.

Their Parts: sympodial and monopodial growth habits, pseudobulbs, foliage, roots and flower spikes, flower parts.

The Living Orchid: respiration, photosynthesis and transpiration.

Buying Plants: adults and seedlings; what to look for.

PART TWO **PLANT CARE AND CULTIVATION**

Their Needs: light and shade, temperatures, water and watering, humidity, feeding.

Flower Care: flower spikes, their flowers and presentation; enjoying your orchids.

Where to Grow Them: In the Home, places and culture.

In the Greenhouse: temperature groups, site and aspect; insulation, staging, heating, shading and ventilation.

Repotting Your First Orchids: why and when, composts, potting procedure; after-care. Rockwool: advantages and culture.

Propagation: divisions, backbulbs, mericlones and seedlings.

Health Care: Pests: slugs and snails, woodlice, mealy bugs, scale insects, spider mites and false spider mites. Diseases: flower spotting, bacterial rot, pseudobulb rot and shrivelling; leaf fall, viruses, non-flowering plants.

PART THREE **POPULAR FIRST ORCHIDS**

Cymbidiums, Paphiopedilums, Miltonias, Odontoglossums, Odontiodas and Phalaenopsis.

Copyright 1993.   The Eric Young Orchid Foundation, Jersey

Printed by The Caxton & Holmesdale Press, Sevenoaks, Kent

Front Cover Flower: Odontoglossum Augres

THE ERIC YOUNG ORCHID FOUNDATION

The late Eric Young VMH, founder of the organisation that bears his name, was one of the last of a long line of major British amateur orchid collectors and growers. His interest in orchids was life-long, and on Jersey between 1958 and his death in 1984 he created one of the finest orchid collections ever held in private hands.

As well as his interest in growing orchids and developing his own collection, he also supported many organisations worldwide with interests in orchid cultivation and research. Projects he supported include the creation of the Eric Young Micropropagation Centre at the Marie Selby Botanic Gardens in Sarasota, Florida, and the funding of a prize to be awarded by the American Orchid Society, for the creation of the first somatic orchid hybrid between two genera that otherwise would not naturally hybridise. He also served on numerous committees, including the World Orchid Conference Committee, the American Orchid Society Research Committee, and for many years on the Orchid Committee of the Royal Horticultural Society, latterly as vice-chairman.

For these and many other services to orchid culture and research he was awarded the Victoria Medal of Honour by the Royal Horticultural Society, the highest honour that organisation can bestow. Throughout his latter years, Eric Young worked to bring about the fulfilment of his dream, that his collection would continue after his death in the form of a Foundation dedicated to the advancement or orchidology. This has come about as the **Eric Young Orchid Foundation** which continues its founder's tradition of breeding and exhibiting fine orchids around the world. Our Founder's prior objective was to persuade as many people as possible to gain his enthusiasm and to enjoy his orchid collection.

Another objective is research into the complexities of hybridising and much has been accomplished in the Laboratory at the Foundation. This work also includes written papers and lectures to the orchid fraternity, including the hobbyist and commercial hybridiser, around the world to share our knowledge with them.

In retrospect this last decade has proved the most successful period in the history of the Eric Young era. The present orchid collection emulates the great Victorian ones when hybrid orchids were fashionable and much in demand. Creating new hybrids and exhibiting them to orchid judging committees around the world is important. The Royal Horticultural Society (RHS) was the first organisation to develop an award system and medals which growers still cherish due to the high standard maintained. Proof of the Foundation's success lies in the number of individual awards gained to-date – six First Class Certificates (the highest accolade for an individual plant) and 133 Awards of Merit.

Displaying groups of orchids has increased over the same period. It is of interest, when entering the Foundation's Display House, the information boards depict the last Gold Medal that Eric Young was to witness at the British Orchid Growers Show in 1982. Since that date four more exhibits have been staged at the Royal Horticultural

2

Society, all receiving the coveted Gold Medal. In 1990, the 'Williams Memorial Medal' awarded to the best exhibit of a single genus of the whole year was given to a display of *Calanthe* at the RHS Halls. In 1991, the 'Lawrence Memorial Medal' which is given to the finest display before the RHS for the whole year was awarded to our exhibit at the Chelsea Flower Show, London.

Exhibiting overseas has not been neglected during this time, showing in many countries such as Germany, France, Italy, USA, and South Africa. During the last decade there have been two World Orchid Conferences, in Japan and New Zealand, and the Foundation staged large exhibits at both in the process winning many international medals.

Alongside exhibiting overseas and in the UK, and the year-round display of orchids provided at the Foundation's nursery at Victoria Village in Jersey, staff from the Foundation also regularly contribute articles to orchid journals, and undertake lecturing trips abroad. In all these respects, the Foundation continues to work in accordance with the principles laid down by its founder, towards the advancement of orchidology, the continuation of the collection's tradition of excellence in the breeding and cultivation of orchids, and the promotion of orchid growing.

Further information about the Foundation can be obtained by writing to:

The Eric Young Orchid Foundation,
Victoria Village,
Trinity, Jersey, JE3 5HH
Channel Islands.

A success story is the breeding of *Phragmipedium* Eric Young which produces a long succession of flowers

INTRODUCING ORCHIDS TO YOU

Well done! In choosing this guide you have opened the door to the royal family of plants. You will discover a wealth of beauty, a variety of flowers and plants unequalled, all within your scope.

Variety is the spice of life and orchids will give it in a lasting and leisurely way. The blossoms come in every colour and combination of hues. Their sizes are also extremely variable, some measuring a few millimetres, the majority several inches and the extra specials seven inches wide. They may be produced singularly or up to two dozen or more as erect, arching or pendant sprays. Shapes are astonishing in variety, from rounded blossoms to others resembling butterflies, spiders, doves, dancers and even monkeys! Some have special intricate shapes and devices to ensure their cross- pollination and value of orchids is the long life of the flowers which few other kinds can equal. Most orchid plants bloom each year, many kinds at different times, and where a modest sized collection is formed it may be possible to have plants in flower all the year round. An extra bonus with many is delicious and unique fragrance.

Variety is also a fascinating feature of orchid plants. Like the flowers they have a great range of sizes, some scarcely an inch high, the majority one to three feet tall and the exceptions up to five feet. Fascinating too is the variety of growth habits. The majority have pseudobulbs, not true bulbs as they are mostly above ground; they may possess a solitary leaf or several. Some kinds are deciduous, shed their leaves before winter, whereas the majority are semi-evergreen. Orchid plants are perennial, that is they live for many years, in some cases over one hundred years!

Altogether there are about 24,000 species, each country of the world possessing some indigenous orchids. Add to this 70,000 hybrids evolved by breeding two species together, choice is unlimited.

Contrary to a misconceived belief that orchids are delicate hot-house plants, the reverse is the truth. They are reasonably tough, needing less attention than many other kinds of plants, and like most people you will eventually discover they are much easier, less demanding to grow to perfection than begonias, saintpaulias, cyclamen and many others. You will discover they need less attention, for example: orchids seldom need watering more than once a week. If they cannot be watered on a routine day they may be left until the next day or several days and will not deteriorate or suffer at all. The tendency is for people to fuss over their first orchids and give them too much attention particularly with regard to watering. They are leisurely in their growth and demands and for this reason are popular with professional people, doctors, politicians and others with varied requirements for their time.

Orchids may be grown in the home, on window-sills or plant tables; outside for a few summer months, in a conservatory, a basement with special lighting, or best of all in a greenhouse. In all cases some heating will be essential.

Wherever you have them, you, your relations and friends will discover a new lasting beauty plus an extremely fascinating magnetic attraction called 'Orchiditis'!

Some words of caution are most necessary when reading about orchids or discussing them with other growers; you may become confused by the different opinions and methods of cultivation. You will discover there are at least a dozen ways of successfully growing orchids. A variety of composts are used and the kinds and amount of fertilisers are many. *DO NOT BE TEMPTED TO MAKE ANY CHANGES UNTIL YOU HAVE ACQUIRED BASIC EXPERIENCE OF GROWING ORCHIDS FOR AT LEAST ONE YEAR.* These plants are by nature leisurely growing; for example, a few months may pass before a first seen flower spike obtains floral perfection. They cannot be forced nor are there any short-cuts to success, particularly through the use of fertilisers. Once you have acquired the basics then fully consider any changes which seem beneficial in other people's methods.

OUR CONCERN IS THAT YOU SUCCEED, THAT YOUR INTEREST DOES NOT FALL AND FAIL WITH YOUR FIRST ORCHIDS, HENCE THE NATURE OF THIS BOOK.

Bold type will emphasise and draw attention to the most important and necessary pointers throughout this publication.

Phalaenopsis is a splendid choice as a first orchid. They will enjoy home or greenhouse culture with plenty of warmth a priority. *Phalaenopsis* Saint Brelades is a superb example of their beauty

5

PART ONE

KNOW YOUR PLANTS

Their Names, Their Parts, The Living Orchid, Buying Plants

When you see orchids or purchase them your query will probably be 'What are their names?' How are orchids identified from other plants?

All kinds of plants are classified into natural orders as families of plants. In the beginning every orchid belongs to the '*Orchis* family' taken from the Greek *Orchus*, but somehow in the course of time orchis became *orchid* and has remained since the earliest years of their history.

Orchids are identified from other plants in that the sexual parts, stigma and stamens, are combined into one common structure called the **column**, and by the development of one of the six floral parts into an unusual, generally strikingly beautiful segment called the **labellum**, **lip** or **pouch**.

According to the structural differences within the families orchids are divided into tribes as **genera** and **species**.

From an orchid enthusiast's point of view there are two base groups, **species**

and **hybrids** and the present day trend is to have some of each in a collection of orchids. And what a choice there is, approximately 24,000 species of orchids which originate from wild natural habitats in most parts of the world, 53 of them in this country. In this book, indeed in most literature concerning orchids, species names are easily recognised by being printed in italics. Each may have two names, sometimes a third. Take as an example *Phalaenopsis amabilis* var. *grandiflora*; the first name applied to this species is the generic one denoting a tribe of related *Phalaenopsis* species. The second name identifies a particular species, *amabilis*; where a species has an outstanding feature it is given a third name, a varietal one, in this case *grandiflora* distinguishing it as having an abundance of flowers (such plants are the exception and not the rule). Species are identified and given names by botanists in all parts of the world.

Orchids from the second group,

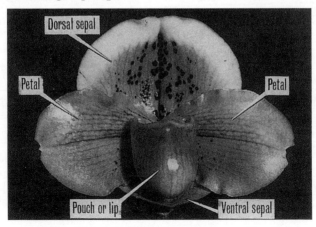

Paphiopedilum Mitzi 'Stonehurst' floral parts identified

Flower parts of *Odontioda* Rozel Bay 'Mont Millais'

hybrids originate from the breeding together of two species. Subsequently hybrids may be mated with a species or with each other. Since the first ever hybrid was made in England and flowered in 1856 we have a choice of 70,000 hybrids. When one of these is created through pollination, raised from the resultant seed and flowered, it is usually named by the originator and together with details of the parentage is registered with the Royal Horticultural Society Orchid Hybrid Registrar. This ensures the names and parentage are exclusive to the originator.

Throughout this book and other literature hybrids are readily recognised since only the *generic (tribal)* name is printed in italics. A typical example is *Phalaenopsis* Gorey 'Trinity'; Gorey is the hybrid name of the *Phalaenopsis* parents (Grouville x Mellor Gold). A further

A popular free flowering species *Phalaenopsis lueddemanniana* originally from the Philippines

cultivar name, enclosed in single quotation marks, may be given to a seedling of special merit, ie 'Trinity', however such names are not included in registrations.

THEIR PARTS IDENTIFIED

Sympodial and monopodial growth, pseudobulbs, foliage, roots, flowers, their parts and long life

As a beginning let us familiarise you with the different parts of orchid plants. Once these are known you will have confidence to discuss or ask questions about orchids; at the same time you will make a worthwhile discovery about one of the fascinations, the variety of shapes and habits.

Sympodial Growth

The construction and habit of orchid growth to a considerable degree indicates their cultural needs. Basically there are two main groups, each with variations within the group. The most common you will meet with, the **sympodial** growth, is easily recognised by a horizontal sometimes ascending **rhizome** (branch), from which the growths are produced. Each year or season the last matured growth (bulb) develops another rhizome and growth; in some kinds the length is scarcely noticeable, in others extending perhaps two or three inches (5 cm or more), which will influence the size of the receptacle in which it grows. Most orchid species and hybrids will develop more than one branched rhizome with growths eventually providing a means of propagation by division. Popular examples of this group are

◄ Commencing with species *Phalaenopsis*, Rosquet Point is the result of several generations of hybridising

cymbidiums, paphiopedilums, cattleyas, odontoglossums and many species.

Monopodial Growth

The other group, orchids with a **monopodial** growth habit, are easily distinguished by having in the place of a rhizome a stem which grows upwards, elongating indefinitely as new stem and leaves are produced at the apex. Branches may be produced from the lower natural main stem, also **aerial roots** from the leaf joints or nodes. Monopodial orchids are not as numerous as other kinds, nevertheless are equally beautiful, the most popular being phalaenopsis and vandaceous kinds.

Pseudobulbs

New growths from the rhizome develop into parts of various sizes and shapes called **pseudobulbs**, but generally most growers call them 'bulbs'. As the name suggests these are not true bulbs, being mostly above the soil or compost, but they are the most exciting, productive part of the plant as it is from these that flowers and new growth buds are produced. Amateur orchid growers spend much of their time just looking at the plants, everything else forgotten, as they look for expected new growths and flower buds, from plants with leisurely responses in both respects. Furthermore the bulbs are the target setters; as they usually produce one bulb each season, which then remains for a few years, they can size up their skills as cultivators according to the improvement noticed. When bulbs get progressively smaller something is lacking and advice is needed.

Pseudobulbs come in all shapes and sizes, most kinds of orchids producing one each year. They may be tall, cane-like, many inches high, or short, squat, oval or rounded ones of various sizes. They may produce a solitary leaf at the apex or more generally several leaves from the tops and sides and the majority are semi-evergreen, some deciduous, shedding foliage before winter. The variety of shapes and sizes is unequalled by any other plant family.

The Foliage

Again variety reigns, not only in their shapes and sizes but in the manner which they are produced as mentioned above. Once you have acquired some experience you will be able to identify the different kinds of orchids according to their foliage and nature of leaf production. Some have long, tough, strap-like leaves (cymbidiums), some thick succulent leaves indicating strong light requirements and less water. The foliage of some are on the thin side (odontoglossums), requiring good shade during the spring and summer. The majority of plants will retain their leaves for two, three or four years, the eldest gradually yellowing during the autumn and winter to eventually fall. This is a natural process and should not incite panic. If all the newer leaves turn yellow there certainly is cause for concern and the need for an inquiry.

You will learn much from the foliage, that it is tougher than generally realised. An impression remains that orchids are delicate plants in need of mollycoddling; the truth is the opposite and our good fortune in choosing orchids is they have the structure and ability to adapt to many different conditions and hardships, and still respond with beautiful flowers.

As the leaves are the main plant powerhouse, converting what the grower provides in the way of good conditions and culture, they should be treated with great respect. Keep them clean with an occasional sponging and most of all ensure they are handled with care to avoid damage through excessive bending, cracking, etc (particularly cymbidiums). Remember they are the lungs of the plants!

The Roots

Generally this is the least seen part of orchids about which it may be commented 'a plant is as healthy as its roots'. A strong root system means strong growth and good flower production. Unfortunately at all times we have to impress and warn that nine out of ten plants which die are the victims of root troubles caused by a failure to understand the roots' requirements, particularly with regard to moisture. Consider then the roots. They need special consideration and understanding as their construction is very different to other kinds of plants and culture of which most will have had experience. Many orchids grown today are **epiphytes** or **semi-epiphytes** which develop a kind of root able to cling to trees or moss-covered rocks; in other words they are plants which grow upon other plants but are not, as often supposed, parasitic. This natural condition is imitated, on a small scale, for some species by attaching them to pieces of tree-fern or bark in which case, like monopodial orchids, they will produce a number of aerial roots. As they require spraying with water this method is not particularly suitable for home orchid culture.

The majority of orchids grown today are, as a result of approximately 140 years of hybridising, far removed from their original natural habitats and are grown very conveniently in pots or similar receptacles in compost. Their roots are thick and covered with a whitish substance called **velamen** capable of absorbing oxygen, carbon

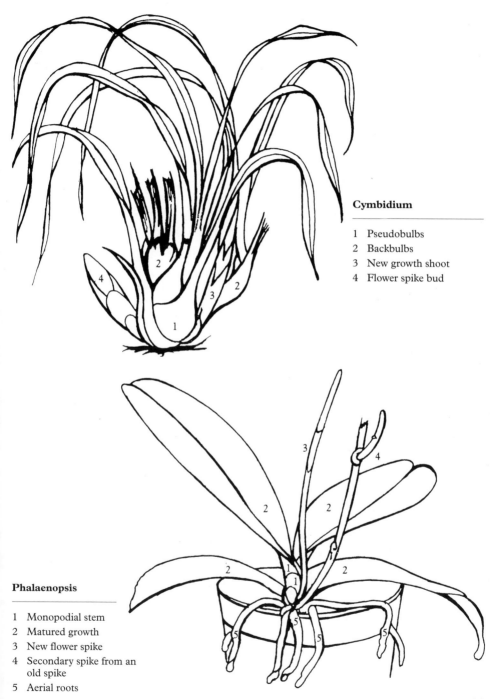

Cymbidium

1 Pseudobulbs
2 Backbulbs
3 New growth shoot
4 Flower spike bud

Phalaenopsis

1 Monopodial stem
2 Matured growth
3 New flower spike
4 Secondary spike from an
  old spike
5 Aerial roots

11

Paphiopedilum

1 Mature growth
2 New growth
3 Old back growth
4 Flower spike
5 Flower bud

Odontoglossum

1 Pseudobulbs
2 Leafless backbulb
3 New growth shoot
4 Leaves
5 Lateral leaves
6 Flower spike

12

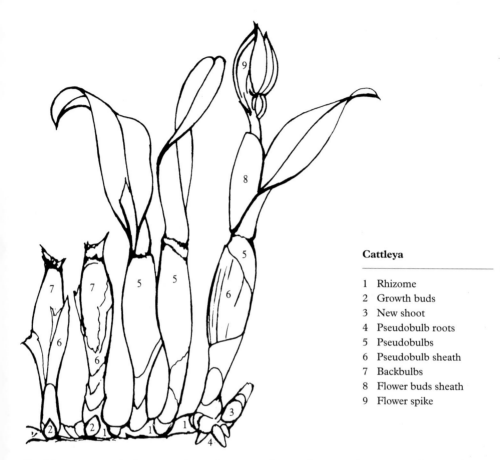

Cattleya

1 Rhizome
2 Growth buds
3 New shoot
4 Pseudobulb roots
5 Pseudobulbs
6 Pseudobulb sheath
7 Backbulbs
8 Flower buds sheath
9 Flower spike

dioxide, water and plant nutrients from orchid composts within the pots. Some roots may stray outside their pots and compost, a freedom which is often beneficial and is indicative of their early origins. The ends of such roots and others will appear jewel-like, of a shiny green colour, when the plants are fully active. When growth and activity lessens during autumn and winter the root tips are enveloped by the white velamen covering and will remain so until the commencement of a new season's growth.

Orchid root systems are scant compared with other plants and seldom exist beyond two or three years. As usual there are exceptions and large strong growing orchids, such as cymbidiums, have extensive vigorous root systems completely enveloping the insides of their pots, a condition called root-bound, and is generally good for the plants. New roots appear at the bases of new growths when they are a few or several inches high, depending on kind, and is followed by a later root-producing period when growth is nearing completion in the autumn.

At this point an appropriate comment is throughout this book, and in conversations with other growers, you will

13

frequently be warned that because of the fleshy nature of orchid roots the main cause of failure with these plants is the destruction of their roots through too frequent waterings.

Flower Spikes

The different plant parts and their numerous variations combine to produce flowers with a greater profusion of deviations in their shapes, arrangements on their stems, and the places from which they appear on the plants. This is the allure of orchids, watching, anticipating and observing the gentle paces of flower development.

Whatever their shape or form the sprays are universally referred to in orchid growers' vocabulary as flower spikes; when first noticed in its early stage it is a **spike**; the plant is in **spike**. Fully developed into a floral display it is a **flower spike**. Depending on kind some are produced from the bases of the pseudobulbs when fully grown and mature; some spikes may appear from the older or previous year's pseudobulbs. Others will be seen inside partly developed new growths, or as in paphiopedilums from within the centres of fully developed growths. Most extraordinary of all are stanhopeas and draculas which have to be grown in open slatted baskets as their spikes are pendulous, issuing from the underneath of the plant. Cane-like pseudobulbs of dendrobiums produce theirs from leaf joints, as do vandas, and the lower growing phalaenopsis (monopodial growth kinds).

Spike development is generally slow. A few months will pass for cymbidium spikes to develop into full flower, indeed this will be true of the majority of orchids. Cattleyas often indicate their intention of flowering by the production of a protective sheath; sometimes these are blind, unproductive, otherwise

several months may pass before they commence to develop fairly quickly into flower.

Long flower life is a foremost attraction of orchids, the majority giving beauty for several weeks, although some last only three or four days. Usually short-lived blossoms possess strong fragrance or odour.

But here is the real joy. With this bonus of flower longevity and a wise selection of a couple of dozen different orchids you will have orchids in flower all the year around!

Flower Parts

At this stage it is necessary to identify the flower parts. There is an outer whorl of three **sepals**, the upper one being called the **dorsal sepal** and is usually the most spectacular in paphiopedilums; the other two may be referred to as the **lateral sepals**. Within the sepals is a circle of three **petals**; the lower one, generally the largest and most colourful, is developed into the **lip** (or **labellum**) or a **pouch** and are specialised to encourage pollinating insects.

At the flower centre there are no obvious stamens and dusty pollen as found in most flowers. Orchids have a single central compound structure known as the **column** bearing at the apex **pollinia** (pollen masses), protected by anther caps; underneath will be found a glutinous cavity known as the **stigma**. The brief description will suffice for the objectives of this book with one exception; if pollinia are dislodged by less then gentle handling, by unwanted visitors such as bumble-bees or mice, pollination will be set in motion. This will explain an often seen premature change of flower colour and loss of blooms.

14

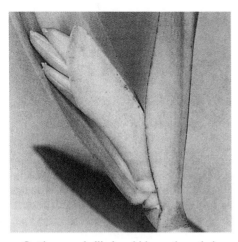

Cattleyas and allied orchids produce their flowers from the tops of the newest matured pseudobulbs

Cymbidiums may produce flower spike buds from the bases of the newest pseudobulbs and/or from the previous ones

Modes of flowering are extremely variable. Paphiopedilums produce their flower spikes from within the centres of matured growth

THE LIVING ORCHID

Respiration, photosynthesis and transpiration

Green fingers are not magic! It expresses where at an early stage people have acquired an affinity with plants. On the other hand there is a tendency to regard plants as 'just plants', giving little if any thought as to how they function. The way to meet their needs and to success is through a feeling and understanding. Think about it! In some respects orchids are like us; they like warmth but not too much of it when, as we do, they become uncomfortable with rapid transpiration. Given too much light they will suffer, perhaps get sunburn. Orchids are unhappy when it is too cold. Applied with too much food or drink we become sick and so will orchids, in fact they may soon die! Moving house and home for us can be stressful and this will be apparent if orchids are often disturbed at the roots, ie repotted more frequently than is desirable. Think about all their needs!

Basically orchids are similar to other plants, each a nature's miracle starting

15

from dust-like seeds. Within the plant is an extraordinary powerhouse involving respiration, photosynthesis and transpiration.

Respiration
Like us plants have to breathe: vaporised air is taken through the **leaf pores** **(stomata)**, the oxygen content extracted for various processes and some carbon dioxide gas is expelled. Respiration is a continuous process, day and night, and draws on a plant's resources according to the ambient conditions.

Photosynthesis
Photosynthesis is a process carried out when prevailing light and temperature are adequate for chloroplasts (which give the foliage green colour), which act like minute solar panels, to combine carbon dioxide with water to make sucrose (sugar), which is used with other nutrients to produce growth, flowering and reproduction. During this process oxygen is expelled to provide the atmosphere we need for living!

Transpiration
Water is absorbed through the roots passed through other parts into the leaves (where all the cells contain water), and is expelled through the pores as water vapour. Depending on the temperature and humidity, 95-99% of the water taken up by the roots is lost to the atmosphere. It is this force, generated by evaporation, that moves dissolved nutrients throughout the plant, mostly during the hours of darkness, and keeps it alive.

These brief descriptions of how plants live will give a strong indication to provide the best situations and environmental conditions for orchids to succeed. This does not normally involve much difficulty; however we do know of cases where people have received their

first orchids, cut off the dead flowers, also all the foliage, kept them in a garage and wanted to know why they were not growing.

BUYING PLANTS
Adults and seedlings and what to look for

Captivated by the beautiful or unusual orchid flowers as they are seen, people are often oblivious of the importance of the plants, their condition and health. The majority of established nurserymen are unlikely to sell an ailing one, but it does happen from time to time. The most likely source of problem plants are private deals or plant auctions and each purchase should be given close scrutiny to avoid disappointment.

Many satisfactory transactions are achieved through selections from catalogues and mail order arrangements however, there are obvious advantages of seeing potential acquisitions in flower as we all have fancies about colours and shapes. Varieties of hybrids and species are priced according to the merits of their flowers and the plants according to their sizes and the numbers of spikes they carry. In the absence of flowers the price is usually low. The same applies if the identification label does not give the whole name, in which case ask for a reduction.

Adults and Seedlings
Your first orchid plant should be an adult one, fully established and capable of bearing more flowers. A source of much interest and speculation once experience has been gained is unflowered seedlings which, depending on their sizes, are less expensive than adult plants. Depending also on their kind seedlings may not flower for two or three years and best

buys are those advertised as 'flowering size' or 'one year to flowering'. The fun and profit of unflowered hybrid seedlings is to some extent unpredictable; you could, when they eventually flower, end up with ordinary varieties, better than average, or a rare meritorious award of merit quality cultivar such as many illustrated in this book. In short it is something of a lottery this sharing of the best pedigree seedlings available!

What to look for

First and foremost is a good sound **root system**. True, these are not generally visible but you should and can ensure a plant is firmly anchored in its compost and pot. Hold a plant by its bulbs or growth and gently tug for looseness (in

Your first orchid is probably one of the popular long-lasting cymbidium hybrids. One of the finest yellows is *Cymbidium* Saint Aubins Bay 'Trinity'

the same way as you would for any pot plant), rejecting those which are not firmly held. This is a sign of a poor root system and a plant is as healthy as its roots!

As a newcomer to orchid growing you will not want to be straightaway involved with **repotting**. Ensure the selected plant has pot and compost space for at least another matured bulb or growth. Another consideration for rejection is if the compost has decayed (although a plant may not have filled its pot with growth), is soft and soil-like; test with a poking-finger. Avoid plants with sprawling growth reaching well over the pot edge. Lovely and interesting they may be but these are for later when experience has been gained.

Cast your eyes over the whole plant to ensure there are no obvious signs of trouble, a lack of foliage, yellow foliage or leaves that have been trimmed. Take into account much shrivelling of the last produced pseudobulb as a warning sign all is not well, particularly if it has not borne any flowers. A reassuring sign of a good plant is the presence of old flower spike stubs.

Consider more closely the foliage. Look for discolorations, blotchy, mottled or streaks of light and dark leaf colours, or black pitting; these are signs of trouble, even serious virus diseases, in which case do not hesitate to reject them.

Fortunately insect pests are few but do not buy them in! (These will be discussed later.) New purchases should be set aside from other plants until you can give them attention, a thorough examination of all parts for pests, and finally cleansing them with a sponging of cool water.

If any defects are noticed bring them to the attention of the nurseryman whose aim will be to give the utmost satis-

17

faction; they will want you to return. When you have been drawn to a beauty of which you have no knowledge, question its suitability to the temperature and cultural conditions you can provide. Insufficient warmth is one of the main causes of failure.

Above all we at the Foundation, and nurserymen, will want your first orchids to be the beginning of a success story.

PART TWO

PLANT CARE AND CULTIVATION

Their Needs, Flower Care and Presentation, Where to Grow Them: In the Home, Greenhouse Culture. Repotting, Propagation, Health Care: Pests, Diseases, Non-flowering Plants

What a worthwhile challenge you have acquired – your first orchids! A challenge? Yes indeed, finding the best place and conditions to encourage the utmost from your treasured orchids. Much will depend on your aims and your means, including the size of your wallet or bank balance. But one thing is certain; you will start in a modest way, perhaps with one plant, to discover orchids are an addiction. Your home orchid growing will often advance to a greenhouse, eventually to be bursting at the seams. You have been warned!

Let us summarise their main cultural needs, then it will follow whereabouts to grow them. Recalling 'How Plants Live' (page 15) we briefly learned the power house was **photosynthesis** dependent on a certain level of **light** and **warmth**; vaporised air (**humidity**) is for the extraction of gases and for plant stability, and **water** most necessary to move dissolved food throughout the plants.

Light and Shade
Orchids (indeed the majority of plants), need certain light levels to produce firm, fine growths and pseudobulbs to bear flowers. Generally it is an insufficiency of

light which inhibits flowering and we must dispel, forget the old idea, that orchids require hot dark humid jungle conditions.

In this country from October to early March orchids will benefit from all available sunshine; from late March to September some form of shading will be necessary for two reasons; to prevent leaf burn and to exercise some control over high inside temperatures which are stressful to the plants. Some kinds will need more shade than others.

Temperatures
Equally important for growth is **warmth** according to how orchids are classified as **cool, intermediate** and **warmth** loving. When beginning do not base the provision of warmth, temperature requirement, on the often quoted **minimum** rather than the **average** one. If orchids are kept at minimum temperature they are seriously handicapped; root moisture and humidity will have to be restricted otherwise there will be other troubles. Another important factor is when the new growing season arrives in the spring, because warmth is based on minimum, the orchids will be later in

18

starting new growth. Temperatures based on the average should be at least five degrees Fahrenheit above the suggested minimum, permitting drop when the weather is cold.

During summer the aims will be opposite, a need to keep the inside temperature below 85°F. Higher temperatures to some extent inhibit growth as when conditions are too hot and dry the leaf pores remain closed and photosynthesis is reduced. As mentioned earlier shading plus ventilation will assist temperature control; however, there will be occasions when it is impossible to keep below the 85°F maximum. Ventilation will be considered in detail under home and greenhouse culture as the means for each are obviously different.

Water
Vital to all forms of life in a plant, water is taken up through the roots to distribute nutrients throughout the system and with another main function of transpiration, 95-99% of the water is passed through the leaves into the air. Water is also required to provide some humidity where orchids are grown.

Supplies
Rain-water is favoured for supplying orchids with root moisture, in other words for watering, as many orchids being epiphytes have evolved very low feed requirements. It is so important that commercial growers and we at the Eric Young Orchid Foundation have invested in enormous facilities for its storage inside the greenhouses and also outside.

Miltonias, the 'Pansy Orchid' are superb pot plants as their life as cut flowers is short. *Miltonia* Jersey 'Trinity' is one of many hybrids raised at the Foundation

Some storage is within the scope of most amateur growers by collecting into water butts or tanks of rain-water from a greenhouse roof or other dwellings to be transferred to the house as needed. It is most necessary that it is warmed to a temperature equal to that of the greenhouse, in most cases between 65°-70°F, before being used for watering.

Unfortunately for the majority, supplies are unlikely to be adequate, particularly during the main growing season; the alternative is local tap-water. This is usually rather high in mineral salts consequently on the alkaline side, whereas a slightly acid or neutral water is preferred for orchids. There is no need to be too concerned as many growers have very good results when they have to use tap-water. One useful part solution when there may be some difficulty in supplying rain-water, when drought is experienced, is to mix the two kinds in equal amounts. A warning: never use water that has been through a water softener.

Watering the Plants

Now we come to the subject which makes the most difference between success and failure. *Be warned: too frequent waterings are the cause of most disasters and disappointments.* Be encouraged: orchids are long-suffering plants and can be restored to good health. Often a beginner cannot control the urge to water because of experiences with other greenhouse or house plants which mostly require frequent waterings. Note

Orchids have several modes of flowering but most unusual, with pendant flower spikes, is *Stanhopea trigrina*, a species from Mexico

'Slipper Orchid' *Paphiopedilum* Saie Harbour 'Trinity' is an example of a first orchid especially for home growing

we emphasise about **too frequent waterings** which is often misinterpreted in other literature and conversations as 'overwatering'. Correctly drained in the pots you cannot give an orchid too much (over water) but you can water it too frequently to create perpetual sodden conditions which is death to orchid roots. As mentioned earlier these are thick compared with other plant roots and if denied air (displaced by the constant presence of water in the air spaces of the compost), they will perish.

Without a healthy root system the remainder of the plant will reveal suffering, through yellowing and subsequent fall of foliage; the pseudobulbs will shrivel and growths weakened until such time as a new set of roots is produced. To a beginner the symptoms may give the impression of being caused through dryness and the situation is worsened by

more waterings! An examination of the root system, by the removal of the plant from its pot, will reveal the truth. If a plant has been denied a sufficiency of watering the roots will still be sound, solid and of whitish colour. If the roots are soft and brown/black in colour, too frequent waterings have taken their toll!

How satisfactory it would be if we could give a definite period for each watering. A host of factors influence, in different ways, the drying of the plant's compost. Pot size has to be reckoned with small ones drying more often than large ones. The age and kind of compost is most influential since generally, as it ages, it holds more moisture for longer. Another factor is the strength of the root system; newly potted plants are allowed longer periods between waterings until new roots have increased. When the compost is filled with roots, a condition

21

known as rootbound which orchids seem to like, more frequent waterings will be needed to meet the demands for moisture. The time of the year, the weather, inside temperatures, the amount of ventilation, and damping-down to create humidity, will influence the need for watering. It follows then the way to success is to consider each plant individually.

Inspections for Watering
Because you have received a gift or bought for yourself a fairly expensive orchid there is a keen sense for its welfare and preservation, a tendency to overdo the requirements. Unfortunately it amounts to mistaken kindness and disappointment. In many ways orchids are plants of convenience which is to your advantage. Particularly is this true of watering. You will set a routine probably for an inspection once each week which is ideal. You will also set aside a certain day. If for some reason this day is inconvenient no harm will accrue if you leave the inspection until the next day or even the following one or longer. What other plant have you grown which permits such convenience? Surprisingly, your orchids will probably be all the better for the delay, indeed it is often said when people are away for a week, even two weeks, without attention their plants come to no harm and may even be better for it! The message to you is orchids need less frequent waterings than is generally supposed.

Cattleyas and related orchids are among the easiest with large glamorous, perfumed flowers such as *Brassolaeliocattleya* Saint Clement 'Trinity', which received the highest RHS award, a First Class Certificate

Watering of orchids will prove to be the most absorbing and satisfying periods of plant growing you are likely to experience. Time will become meaningless as you handle each orchid in turn to accurately assess its needs. You will observe the progress of its growth, when nearing maturity how much larger it may be than the previous growth or psuedobulb (not smaller we hope!), or the appearance of a new spike. It is is an exciting part of orchid culture.

The important decision you will have to make regarding the need for watering will be undertaken with confidence after a few weeks of experience. You will be dealing with a compost of bark pieces, peat, a mixture of the two with white perlite added for drainage, or perhaps your plants are growing in a greyish woolly substance known as 'Rockwool', a newish medium. The surfaces may look dry but it could be sufficiently moist underneath (a darker colour) a condition ascertained by carefully delving into the compost with the fingers; however such disturbance carried out regularly will be undesirable and unnecessary as your experience increases. You will be able to rely on the professional way judging by the feel, the weight of each plant, whether it lifts 'light or heavy'. In the beginning make a determined effort to differentiate between light and heavy by frequent testing, making comparisons with plants which are heavy immediately after watering. Yes, you are right; some will be in different size pots or the plants are larger or smaller which creates a degree of difficulty in the beginning. Getting the feel for each and every one is a knack which will soon follow with experience.

Cautions

Above all be certain the compost in the pot is dry before watering. Always remember **if in doubt leave watering out**, not until the next day but until the next inspection. Never assume because the compost is considered not quite dry it needs just a little water. Frequent dribblings lead to unwanted complications, wet on top and dry underneath, or the whole is saturated causing decay of the roots.

When watering is considered necessary use water that is approximate to the temperature requirement of the kind of orchid, or more generally, approximately 65°F (19°C), never above this temperature. Following nature's way pour water on to the compost from above and all round the surface, not just in one place as orchid composts usually have free drainage, water runs straight through. Ensure all the compost is wetted until it passes through the pot drainage holes. Watering-cans with a slightly bended spout are advantageous as is one with a small outlet to give complete control, otherwise some water may find its way into growths; if unnoticed and it remains inside for some time it may cause damping-off (rot). Accidents do occur in which case turn the victim plant upside-down to release the water: blow into the growth to be doubly sure.

Occasionally water may not readily penetrate the compost surface due to excessive dryness. If after a minute or two it has disappeared giver another application, or two, until the dryness has been cured. If the condition persists immerse the plant up to its pot rim in a bowl or bucket of water until air bubbles cease to rise.

Humidity

A certain amount of moisture (water vapour) in the atmosphere is required for healthy growth and is generally referred to as 'relative humidity'; in other words the amount of water the air may hold according to the temperature. The higher the latter the greater the amount of moisture it may hold; conversely as this air cools less moisture is required to maintain relative humidity until a point is reached when it becomes saturated. This has to be avoided for the good of the orchids.

A humidity gauge will give some guidance as to relative humidity but are not entirely dependable regarding accuracy. In time a grower will get the 'feel' for the right conditions: if comfortable for you, comfortable for your plants.

The ideal requirement is between 40-60% relative humidity and is created by damping-down, spraying water over the greenhouse floor and paths. During the main growing season, on sunny days between March and September, in most situations this will mean damping-down in the morning and in the afternoon. When a day is very hot, the air dry, humidity may be increased by giving the plants a light misting with rain-water. On a dull day one damping-down may be sufficient. In winter once or twice a week may suffice at all times depending how much artificial heat is needed to maintain temperatures. If during inclement weather these are very low it is advisable to keep the surroundings on the dry side.

Feeding Orchids

Associated with watering is their nutrient requirement which is less than required for most other plants. Recapping on 'The Living Orchid (page 15) we emphasised their leisurely pace of growth and flower spike development and now warn that any attempt to force orchids with fertilisers may have the opposite affect – disaster! The truth is many orchids will do quite well without the application of fertilisers. On the other hand results can be improved with modest feeding from spring until the end of summer. During

winter when days are short and light generally poor, even if producing flowers the plant's growth and activity is at its lowest ebb, *its least active state*; its roots will also be quiescent.

Fertilisers are rarely applied directly to the orchid composts when it is changed at repotting. Liquid or soluble powder nutrients are generally used as routine feeding. There are many kinds available which are suitable though not specifically prepared for orchids. Each will carry an analysis of the nutrient content and at this stage it will suffice to know the three major elements **nitrogen (N)**, **phosphorus (P)** and **potash (K)** will be quoted in this order and a given ratio, eg N.30, P.10, K.10; or N.20, P.10, K.10; or N.10, P.10, K.10; in the first two more nitrogen than the other elements. Since bark composts are widely favoured, the higher nitrogen will be ideal, as they are lacking in this nutrient. Also quoted in smaller quantities will be trace elements which are necessary for plant growth. In other words most general liquid and powder fertilisers, although mainly intended for tomatoes, pot plants etc, will be ideal for orchids *diluted to half recommended strength*. Those especially prepared as 'Orchid Fertilisers' are applied according to their instructions (without dilution).

From March onwards until the end of September feeding is included as general watering procedures, but **importantly each third watering should be without fertiliser**. Sufficient should be applied to flush all the compost and water seen flowing through pot drainage holes. The objective is to ensure there is not any build-up of fertiliser strength in the compost as this will be detrimental, indeed poisonous to our plants. Always remember an orchid will only take in

A typical wood-framed amateur's orchid house. Note on the left side upper roof lath blinds for shading and water butt for collecting rain-water

Box vents set in the side walls allows passage of cool air into the lower parts, eventually towards the roof vents, creating gentle air movement

what it needs from the compost. Little and often is a good beginning for your first orchids.

Another important factor to bear in mind is the quality of the light reaching the plants. There is a tendency to over-shade greenhouses and providing good light is the prevailing difficulty of growing orchids in the home, neverthe-less it is not insurmountable. Good light fuels orchid living; without it and photosynthesis feeding is of little benefit to growth.

25

FLOWER CARE

Flower spikes, presentation, cut flowers and enjoying your orchids

Not so many years ago orchids were seasonal in flowering, the summer being the least floriferous. Today as a result of the work of hybridists we enjoy a wealth of flowers all the year round reaching a peak during winter and spring. Since many orchids flower at the same time each year, often within a matter of days, we will know when to start looking for the flower spike bud. Many weeks will pass before they reach full flowering, weeks of anticipation requiring some extra attention and care.

It is logical for owners of their first orchids with flower spikes to assume the plants will need more water and nutrient. This is not the case since there is sufficient reserve to produce their flowers; *watering should be normal without any extras.*

A warning of occasional disappointment is necessary as now and then a plant may start spike production, even to the flower bud stage, to fail. This is usually because a plant has insufficient size, strength and reserves, to fulfil its ambitions. In some cases it is advisable to give preference to growth by nipping out spikes at an early stage when plants are lacking in size. Young seedlings, propagations, or ailing plants, will benefit from such consideration, hard though it may be!

When flower spikes are discovered it will be found helpful to mark their presence, at an early age, with a slim neat cane, pushing it into the compost near to the new spike and at the pot edge. If the requirement is for a fairly tall one (such as for cymbidiums), place a small flower pot on the top of the cane to prevent a serious poke in the eye.

Flower presentation is more spectacular if the spikes are given a suitable unobtrusive support. Once trained the cane is shortened just above the tie, in this case a phalaenopsis

Flower Presentation

Now to the tying and training of flower spikes, the method depending on the kind of orchid. Miniature varieties and pendulous spikes are unlikely to require support. The majority however will need some support and in many cases you will have the added pleasure of choosing an arched, curved spike, or an erect one. The former is achieved by one supporting tie to a cane below the first flower bud, the remainder of the spray allowed to shape into a natural curve through weight. Should there be a long spray and many flowers a second cane and tie will be needed approximately two-thirds along the length of the spike to prevent breakage through sheer weight. An erect spike may need two or three ties, one below the first flower bud and others at

26

Most cymbidium flower spikes will need support, the first tie positioned near the base, followed much later with a second tie just below the flower buds

Without a support and tie, paphiopedilums rarely lift up their faces to be fully appreciated

A neat cane and tie support lifts the flower to perfection

intervals between the flower buds, as the spike develops, to train an erect stance. In all cases tying should be delayed until such time as the stem has acquired a degree of hardness, stiffened, as any attempt at tying while young and tender will end in disaster, a twisted or snapped off spike.

Paphiopedilums (slipper orchids) will need a short supporting cane with a single tie just below the individual flower bud, to lift up the 'faces' when the flowers are fully developed. To appreciate the unusual beauty of these flowers, where possible raise their height to eye level; standing them on an upturned flower pot is often sufficient.

Remember to return all spike-bearing plants to their same positions with the spikes in their original direction, otherwise those with several flowers will be disarranged, facing in different directions.

Beautiful species *Aërides lawrenceana* is an example of monopodial growth with an upright stem

Appreciate Your Orchids

Mostly their will give many weeks of pleasure, will be conversation pieces, in a home either as a solitary pot plant or as a focal point of beauty in an arrangement of plants. If the preference is for a large display in a bowl with foliage plants, ferns, ficus, pepperomias, etc, they are planted in the solid as permanent; orchid plants are best left in their pots bedded in the soil in which case they are readily replaced when the flowers fade.

Your first orchid may have started in this fashion and how long the flowers will live depends on their positions in a home; not too near sources of heat (on a TV or near a lighting source!), out of draughts, direct or strong sunshine. If they are

Paphiopedilum Maudiae with highly attractive foliage is a typical sympodial growth orchid

placed in a second container (bowl), containing pebbles and water to create some humidity, the enjoyment will be for longer. In the end, when the blossoms change colour and curl, the spike should be cut near its base leaving a short stub. Some orchids, such as the popular in-home phalaenopsis, will give a second branch display of flowers if part of the spike, about two-thirds, is allowed to remain; cut the top portion, when the flowers are finishing, just above a node joint (swellings along the stem). However, if your plant has less then four leaves cut back to the base of the spike.

Cut orchid flowers may last in perfect condition for several weeks placed in water which is changed each three or four days; a fresh stem cut each time helps to prolong flower life. Most important to longevity will be maturity of all the flowers before the spike is cut. If a single flower (a paphiopedilum for example), it needs to have been fully open for two to three weeks before it is cut. Where a spray of several flowers is concerned cutting should be delayed until the last developed flower has enjoyed two or three weeks of perfection. It is all about what experienced growers call 'substance of the flower'. Try it yourself; test its thickness by feeling gently between a thumb and finger. Some of the longest lasting flowers will possess a cardboard-like thickness (as in cymbidiums, paphiopedilums, etc).

WHERE TO GROW THEM

In the home, in the greenhouse

How your interest in orchids was kindled can be categorised into two main groups (1) as a gift; (2) attracted to them at a flower shop, a garden centre, botanical and other large gardens, in amateurs' collections, or by reading.

The first group will cause the most concern and anxiety since **gift orchids** are unprepared for and are seldom accompanied by concise instructions for their care and subsequent cultivation. Cymbidium and phalaenopsis, the most likely gift orchids, are produced and marketed in vast quantities, at present mainly from Holland or Denmark. Cymbidiums, because of their robust plant size and many flowers appear the most attractive, but the lovely phalaen-opsis are more accommodating in size, and with their liking for house tempera-tures and less available light, are especi-ally ideal for indoor culture. Unfor-tunately your benefactors were not aware of these facts and the choice is generally in favour of cymbidiums, maybe because of a casual sales comment they do not require much heat and they are easy. We can only hope that in the absence of a greenhouse or conservatory you will enjoy your first cymbidium and then look at other kinds of orchids.

What do you do with your first gift orchid, the cymbidium, once the flowers are removed? Until June they will need indoor protection with average warmth of 55°-60°F (12.8°-15.6°C); otherwise rising to 85°F (29.4°C). They will need a position of good light, a southerly window-sill with the shading of net or light curtains, or better still a temporary home in a sun-porch. About mid-June, when good outside temperatures are likely, cymbidiums may be placed outside, in a garden, where shaded by a tall tree or building for the hot midday hours; otherwise some light shading will have to be arranged. About early October, or sooner if there is a danger of hard frost, cymbidiums are returned to their former inside positions. The aim, and herein lies the difficulty, should be to provide adequate warmth, about 55°F (12.8°C), and after flowering to provide light, to start the new growths in time to have a long growing season so as to reach maturity by the beginning of October. Otherwise there will be few if any flower spikes, unhappily a common complaint where there are not the appropriate facilities to accommodate cymbidiums.

The second group of first time owners will more likely and wisely have the benefit of some advice in advance of purchases. To see orchids in cultivation is a tremendous advantage, particularly if it is an amateur's situation with the benefit of the experience of having started with their first orchids behind them.

IN THE HOME

Situations, window-sills, growing cabinets, special needs and which kinds

Compared with greenhouse culture, indoor orchid growing is a greater challenge because of the difficulty of providing conditions best for growth and flowering. Even so thousands of people have succeeded, those who relish a challenge and love the beauty of these flowers. There are even advantages of indoor orchids; the plants are mostly under constant observation (in a greenhouse it is often limited to an hour or two each day), and homes provide ideal warmth to suit most kinds of orchids. It is often said 'if you are comfortable the

orchids are too!' and we are generally very comfortable in our homes!

The key to successful indoor orchid growing is discovering the right place offering *good light* for each kind of orchid, particularly as the light source will be from one direction and not from all round as in a greenhouse. If warmth is readily available but light inadequate there will be problems of poor floppy growths and non-flowering.

Cymbidium devonianum, with pendant flower sprays, will succeed suspended in a window site with good light

30

A tea-trolley is very useful for accommodating orchids in a home; they can be moved away from windows during hot sunshine or nearer to warmth on cold nights

Home situations are extremely variable, as a consequence there may be exceptions to the general comment and advice which follows. Whether old or modern, centrally heated or otherwise, aspects in relation to the sun, will all create numerous variations. Very few orchids will enjoy the same light-lacking conditions which are adequate for many foliage house plants, for example on a dresser or sideboard far away from a window. Window-sills or positions near

31

THREE EASILY GROWN ORCHIDS FOR HOME CULTURE

Extremely popular today are orchids of lesser size and a lovely example for a cool house or the home is *Dendrobium cuthbertsonii*, a free flowering species from the Far East

Top right: Many other kinds will flourish with odontoglossums and *Miltonia spectabilis* var *moreliana* is sure to succeed

Lower right: Cattleya and allied species are popular, especially *Laelia gouldiana*, a plant of moderate size, autumn flowering, and suitable for indoor culture

Another splendid orchid for indoors is
Phalaenopsis equestris, a species with a long
flower season

Paphiopedilum appletonianum with mottled
foliage will enjoy the warmth of a home which
is usually around 65°-70°F

them will be the main places for successful orchid growing.

Windows with a south aspect will
receive the strongest light necessitating
some shading for all but the winter
months to prevent scorch and excessive
temperatures (85°F or more). East and
west aspects will allow early morning or
late evening sunshine which is good and
the remaining daylight period will suit
many kinds. A few orchids will do
reasonably well in a north-facing window, one without any sunshine, and is of
course the coolest.

Shapes and sizes of window-sills will
be variable, and will influence the size
and numbers which may be grown without overcrowding and in competition for

available light. Horizontal glass shelving
is one solution to population explosion,
with interspaces between shelves to cope
with different plant sizes. Another
possibility is casing a window recess with
glass to improve growing conditions,
particularly humidity, however with
means of ventilation for temperature
control. One situation, however, which
must be avoided is shutting out the
orchids, denying them vital warmth at
certain seasons, by drawing curtains.

Another versatile method of accommodating orchids is on a tea-trolley,
usually two-tiered, which can be moved
away from a window during very hot
sunny periods. Plant poles extending
from floor to ceiling, with adjustable

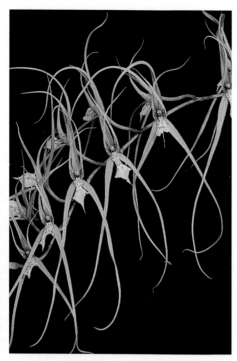

The unusual spectacular *Brassia verrucosa* will be found to be easy going in most situations including in the home

Restrepia guttulate is another fascinating dwarf orchid suitable for home culture

plant holders, is another attractive way of keeping orchids. Whatever the method and ingenuity *remember the vital requirement is good light.*

Growing Cabinets

Increasing in popularity are various types of glass enclosures, the most sophisticated often referred to as 'planteriums'. These are variable in style, size and equipment. The majority require considerable cash outlay as usually cabinets are designed and produced by individual highly skilled craftsmen; rarely are they mass produced. The best are the equivalent of a fully automated greenhouse where plant needs are computer controlled; just plug into an electricity supply to obtain day and night periods with artificial light, warmth and humidity, plus a gentle flow of air within the cabinet. They can and often are a special beautiful feature within a home for the display of flowering orchids from a greenhouse and may include a small landscape scene which utilises tree pieces, a rock or two, and some foliage plants. Or the ultimate could be a complete growing room, in a basement for example, with the installation of fluorescent-type lights developed specifically for growth; these will also provide sufficient warmth. But first acquire some experience with your orchids.

Special Considerations, Particularly Humidity

With experience you will develop special tricks for meeting the needs of orchids, particularly creating humidity which is

35

most difficult to provide in a home without damaging the furnishings. In a greenhouse humidity is raised simply by spraying water on the floors and during very hot weather misting over the plants.

Indoors it is beneficial to accommodate several plants together on a tray not only to assist humidity but for the convenience of handling the plants if they are taken elsewhere for watering. The trays are provided with about one inch depth of shingle or gravel which is kept almost covered by water which evaporates and provides humidity. Some arrangement, such as wire on steel mesh, to stand the plants on is necessary so that they are not in contact with the wet gravel to set up a capillary action which will result in constant 'wet feet' orchids; this must be prevented if the plants are to thrive.

Light spraying or mistings over the top of the plants, allowing the moisture to float down on them, will assist growth in the generally drier conditions of a home and be most beneficial when temperatures are high. Rain-water should be preferred to tap-water which often leaves white chalky deposits on the plants.

A place may be found in a home, where there is good light, for most kinds of orchids, *Laelia anceps*, a variable species, is a popular subject

One of the easiest is *Stenoglottis longifolia* which from a rosette of foliage produces tall spikes of many dainty flowers during the autumn and winter; it is a good window-sill orchid

Which Kinds

Whether species or hybrids, those with moderate light requirements will prove the best for indoor culture. Most popular are phalaenopsis, paphiopedilums, particularly the mottled foliage ones, odontoglossums and odontiodas which prefer cool conditions, and the showy miltonias (pansy orchids). These are some of the best starter plants. Among the more difficult are species attached to pieces of tree-fern or cork-bark and other orchids with many aerial roots; good humidity and sprayings at least two or three times a day are needed to encourage the best from them.

Although generally less flamboyant than hybrids, species will provide endless fascination often combined with unique beauty and are just as easy to grow. Choice is tremendous even if limiting your selection to smaller plants and avoiding those with awkward straggling growths. If there are any doubts about the suitability of a species for your conditions ask the supplier; all of them in this country have a reputation of being genuine and eager to please.

37

A from floor-to-ceiling high plant pole is another convenient way of growing orchids successfully in a home. Phalaenopsis seen here are enjoying their situation

Site and aspect temperatures, insulation, staging, heating, shading and ventilation

Temperature Groups

When considering accommodation for your first orchids, nature smiles on us very kindly for in our favour, to give much encouragement, is the extraordinary resiliency and ability of orchids to adapt to a variety of situations and conditions. Given sufficient time (most important), they will flourish. A not unusual situation is a greenhouse where other kinds of plants are in the majority, including the popular tomatoes. One question that has to be answered is will there be sufficient warmth forthcoming at all times of the year for your orchids in a mixed plant house? In this regard we have to consider the ideal temperature requirement, when heat has to be provided, for the different kinds of orchids which may be placed in three basic groups:

(1) **Cool:** when the ideal temperature should be 50°-55°F (10°-12°C) at night (the coldest period), rising at least 5°F by day if artificial warmth is needed. In this group will be cymbidiums, odontoglossums, odontiodas, masdevallias and various species.

(2) **Intermediate:** ideal temperature 57°-62°F (14°-17°C) at night rising at least 5°F by day. This group contains the largest selection of kinds including paphiopedilums, phragmipediums, cattleyas and allied orchids, lycastes and anguloas, oncidiums, coelogynes, epidendrums, dendrobiums and many others.

(3) **Warm:** ideal temperature 64°-68°F (18°-20°C) at night rising to 70°F (21.1°C) by day. In this group will be the popular and widely grown phalaenopsis and mottled leaved paphiopedilums.

Earlier we warned about the problems of inadequate warmth; this is not within the adaptability of orchids. The opposite fortunately is that many kinds will adapt to warmer conditions than their group indicates as usually there are parts of a greenhouse which are warmer (or cooler). Similarly this is also applicable with regards to shade requirements, some parts being darker than others or taller plants will give shade.

Whatever the situation it is a fairly safe bet that eventually orchids will take over completely. Let us consider then a greenhouse for orchids.

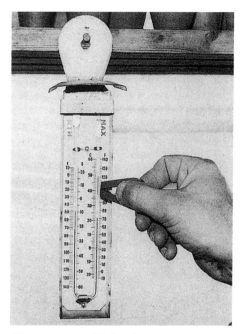

Thermometers which register maximum and minimum temperatures are most necessary as it is important to know about warmth during your absence

Greenhouses

Any kind of house, whether span-roofed, three-quarter span, or lean-to or dome shaped will, if heated, be suitable for orchid culture. And there is a great variety to choose from, varying in the kind of structural material, glass sizes, ventilation, and staging arrangements etc. Most amateur orchid growers prefer an equal span-roof type ten to twelve feet in length, an eight foot width which allows a three foot wide central pathway and two foot six inches wide plant benches each side. Ridge height is usually nine to ten feet and sides six feet (from ground to eaves). If a greenhouse is devoted entirely to orchids, with benches three feet high, half of the sides above the benches should be glass and the lower remainder of brick or wood. If the house is to be a dual purpose one, ie for tomatoes, cucumbers, pot plants and orchids, one side of the house has to be all glass to ground to accommodate and grow tomatoes successfully.

Should the choice be a metal or wood structured house? It is an almost toss-a-coin situation. Metal framed, usually of light alloy, have a longer life and little maintenance requirement. Deal or pinewood will need regular painting or the more expensive cedar wood houses will require a preservative treatment each two or three years. Weigh against this the fact that wood is a better heat retainer and the house approximately 5°F warmer plus the ease and lower cost of making fixtures and insulations, wooden structures are often preferred.

Site and Aspect

First and foremost is the siting of the greenhouse in relation to the main

39

building. Aside from the necessity to be near to the main services, electricity, water, etc, a house should be near to your home and not at the bottom of a garden. It is certain there will be numerous times when you will be visiting the orchid house, even at night, when there is a special flower spike developing or slugs to be destroyed, or for relaxing reasons; there will be many visits! A greenhouse situated lengthwise south to north gives a little advantage in that during the summer, with the sun shining along the length of the house, the inside temperature will not be as high as when the sun shines directly into the interior from the south as in an east to west aspect. As previously stated, high temperatures above 85°F are not desirable, though at times impossible to prevent. Siting should not be in the proximity of tall buildings or trees which may cast shade for more than an hour or two.

Insulation-reduced Costs

Glass double glazing is undoubtedly superior but too expensive for the majority of growers who will resort to fitting an inside 'skin' of polythene. How influential this will be in reducing heating costs depends on the efficiency of outside glazing and fixture of the polythene with at least a one to two inches (2.5°-5° cm) air gap. This trapped layer of air forms the actual insulation. A more recent skin polythene known as 'bubble sheeting' is gaining popularity in spite of cutting down even more light to the plants. As the name suggests it is a double skinned polythene with sealed bubbles of air and is obtainable in two bubble sizes; the larger one is less obstructive to light. The slight loss of light of inner linings does not appear to affect growth, consequently linings are generally left in position all the year round until such time (several years),

40

there is a noticeable deterioration in the light transmission due to discoloration with age of the polythene. When fixing ventilators need to be lined separately to allow their operation.

Cleanliness of the outside glass and the inner polythene lining is most essential to ensure the orchids receive the maximum available light which is often low and of short duration during winter.

Plant Benches and Staging

For many years a double staging, a lower bench containing a moisture retentive aggregate under the upper staging for the plants, was considered the norm. From the 1950s onwards a single slatted staging was generally accepted as more beneficial and conducive to healthy growth in smaller houses, and of course, are less expensive to install. Open slatted staging allows free circulation of air and warmth all round the house, through the plants, with atmospheric moisture gathered mainly from the wet floors below. This method has much to commend it when heating is supplied by an electric fan heater positioned on the floor. Good air circulation eliminates problems which occur with stagnant overmoist conditions.

Useful ferns and other foliage plants which do not require much light may be grown in pots on the floor under the orchid benches. Floor soil is best covered with a one inch layer of pea-beach pebbles which is kept wet by damping-down (spraying) with water to provide humidity. Do not allow the foliage plants a dense growth situation which may encourage slugs: thin out the plants from time to time when they will prove valuable additions as house plants in the home.

Two feet square concrete slabs laid upon the floor soil so as to be an inch or so above the general level will provide a

Interior of an amateur's orchid house. Shelving, well above the benches, are suitable for orchids requiring more light and warmth. Note the inner 'skin' of polythene for insulation

good walkway; it is also wetted when damping-down.

Heating for Small Houses

For your first orchids an electric fan heater of three kilowatt size will be ideal for providing warmth up to 65°F (18.3°C) in a ten by eight foot house. There are lesser power models of 2-2.5 kW, however it is wiser to have some spare capacity than to have a heater constantly called upon to maintain temperatures.

Choose a heater designed for a greenhouse rather than a domestic one as the former usually has a constant fan running facility in addition to fan action when warmth is demanded by an inbuilt thermostat. As to the cost of heating, a useful calculation to bear in mind is that each increase of 5°F in temperature doubles the electricity bill.

Fan heaters are best placed about one metre from a corner of a house, underneath the plant staging, on two or three building bricks so as to be three to four inches above floor level. Because of the damp inside conditions, follow installation instructions supplied with the apparatus or consult an electrical engineer if there are any doubts. Take no risks!

Paphiopedilums, Slipper Orchids, are excellent for home growing. Classical *Paph* Mont L'Abbé 'Trinity' AM/RHS is in flower for many weeks

Paphiopedilum Lynleigh Koopowitz 'Trinity' has an Award of Merit (AM/RHS) from the Royal Horticultural Society as have many other orchids illustrated

Splendid subjects for home culture are paphiopedilums and a good example is *Paph* Pinocchio
which produces a succession of blooms over several months

Alternatives, depending to some extent on the location of a greenhouse, could be plumbing into a domestic hot water pipe system of a residence, gas or oil heaters.

Thermometers

The most important item of equipment you will need is a thermometer which registers maximum and minimum temperatures. Knowledge of what happens to the temperature during your absence will in the beginning be extremely helpful towards providing the ideal conditions at all times for your orchids. Needles inside glass stems on each side of a thermometer, one for maximum and other for minimum, are each day drawn down with a magnet to the mercury levels, to be moved according to the temperature. To obtain the most useful readings the positions of thermometers is important. Note the plural; even in a small greenhouse there will be some differences of temperatures in positions which may be used to advantage. Some orchids will appreciate a little less warmth than others, therefore a couple of thermometers, in different positions, are a good investment.

These should be positioned among the plants and not in open space above a pathway for convenience of reading and where at certain times the thermometers are subjected to sunlight to give false impressions.

Shading and Ventilation

During a growing season temperature control is linked to a joint application of shading and ventilation, particularly in hot weather when the objective is to keep the inside reading around 85°F (29.4°C). In a small volume of air such as a ten by eight foot house changes, may be more frequent and rapid than those of commercial houses from which your plants originated with large capacities. On hot days, depending on the siting of an orchid house, prompt action is often necessary to prevent an early rise in temperature; once it becomes very high it is very difficult to reduce it until late in the day.

Shading of some density will be needed from March to September, how much and when depending on the kind of orchid. Various methods may be employed; the ideal ones, unfortunately the most expensive, are lath blinds which are rolled in position or removed according to the weather. A less costly and equally effective method involves the use of a shade cloth, as blinds, with each end attached to a roller.

Most crucial will be the density of the shade. Although the main objective is to control temperatures too much shading generally inhibits good growth and flowering. Consider then the shade

requirement of your first orchids. With inside polythene bubble-type insulation permanently in position there is already some shade. With the first period of bright sunshine in February there is no need for panic and hasty application of shading. Only when the weather is settled will it be necessary to have blinds in position for the brightest period of the day. Generally by mid-March, if you are absent at business and have previously noted the inside temperature has risen to near 85°F (29.4°C) without blinds there is no cause for alarm as the period would have been a short one. April onwards will require full shading until the end of August when it is again reduced gradually, introducing the plants to full light.

Small greenhouses, because of a volume difference, tend to become more stuffy than larger ones but to some extent this may be overcome with adequate ventilation. The main purpose of shading however, will be to exercise control over temperatures as previously mentioned.

Standard **ventilation** in most greenhouses is **roof vents** on each side of the roof. These are generally fitted with automatic open and shut equipment which is set according to temperature requirement; otherwise manual levers, easily fitted, are available from most greenhouse manufacturers. Side ventilators, which of course are usually at plant level, are not favoured for orchid culture as the air admitted at this point is drying to the plants and diminishes humidity. Roof top ventilators are excellent since hot air, which rises and collects in the upper regions, is released. **Box ventilators,** built into the lower side wall (seldom provided in standard general greenhouses), are a valuable asset well worth installation. Opened in conjunc-

44

Cool greenhouse orchids are divided into two groups, those which require much shade and others with cymbidiums in the majority in need of strong light. *Cymbidium* Gorey is a superb example of the standard cymbidiums

tion with the roof vents they create a gentle flow and exchange of air, at the same time assist temperature control on hot days. **Extractor fans**, in a high position, are also very effective in removing hot air, but are not essential for small greenhouses if there are sufficient roof vents on each side.

To be effective on potentially hot days ventilation needs to be applied early before the inside temperature has risen many degrees. At times during summer, for cool and intermediate orchids, the vents are left open to some extent all night. In addition to preventing early morning rises in temperature, night ventilation will often be necessary to impose lower readings at night at least 5°F less than day. This is important not only for the well being of the plants but also for flower production.

If your fan heater does not have a fan only facility, air circulation needs to be improved with an independent fan. One which causes some movement of the plants' foliage will be ideal and needs to be in daily operation during the growing season, even at night when there are close conditions.

To put your minds at rest, yes there will be occasions when it will be impossible to prevent the greenhouse temperature rising above the desirable 85°F. Keep the inside moist when you can, and spray overhead, then at night ensure the orchids enjoy cooler conditions. All will be well!

Once established, having grasped and experienced the *basic needs* and management of orchids which we have given, you will no doubt wish to aspire to better things. The best move you can make is

Miltoniopsis will also enjoy odontoglossum conditions or even on a window-sill, providing the light is not too strong. *Mil* Augres 'Trinity' is one of many hybrids available today

into automation particularly if you are frequently absent for long periods. Overhead and under bench spraying, with automatic controls and timers will be well worthwhile. In the meantime if possible keep a full greenhouse, even include other kinds of plants as this is invaluable in producing good growing conditions. A few orchids on their own are rarely happy!

REPOTTING YOUR FIRST ORCHIDS

Composts, potting procedure, after-care and rockwool

Why and When to Repot

If your first orchid was a gift originating from a garden centre there is no telling its condition or its requirements for repotting without examination. If, more fortunately, it came from an orchid nurseryman, you bought it directly, it is unlikely it will need repotting for at least a year (a factor worth bearing in mind when selecting plants). Two conditions will influence why and when an orchid needs repotting. Some may need it annually, the majority will last a couple of years, and a few even longer. The first decisive condition concerns space for a plant's development; when growths have reached the pot rim more space is needed. The second concerns the state of the compost, how much it has decomposed and needs replacing. This may be ascertained by prodding with a finger; if it is very soft, gives way to pressure, is soil-like, repotting is necessary.

Usually the question of repotting arises when a gift orchid has finished flowering. If it does need attention the ideal time will be when new growth shoots are three to four inches high (depending on kind), and is likely to occur anytime between February and September. Otherwise, unless a plant's condition is serious, repotting should be deferred until the ideal period. Some orchids, such as the popular phalaenopsis which do not produce new growth shoots but an extension of its centre, are repotted during the same period when new roots are seen, the best sign of activity.

Their Composts

Regardless of the origin of your orchids, as their numbers increase cultivation will be easier if all are provided with the same compost; then you will not have to deal with a variety of conditions, each with different water requirements and frequency of drying. Yes, there are several varying composts; because of their fibrous lumpy nature they are rarely referred to as soil, and producers and amateur growers have their different recipes, but for your early experiences we stay with the basic ones.

Orchid composts have to be long lasting so as to avoid frequent repotting, well drained yet with some moisture retentive quality because of the orchid root construction, and provide sufficient nutrient for growth. The main components are organic, peat and fir-bark, with perlag or a similar lightweight aggregate to assist aeration. At the present time such mixtures are very popular but in more recent years a new inorganic medium 'rockwool' has proved successful for some orchids with several advantages

47

over organic composts. Since your first orchids may be in rockwool, this will be dealt with separately.

Conveniently, orchid composts are readily available in small quantities either direct or by mail order from orchid nurserymen or sundriesmen. State the number, size and kind of orchid you need to repot. Generally you will receive exactly the same compost mix as the producer uses for their plants. Some may even offer a repotting service.

A good quality bark mixture with some added perlite is preferred for most kinds

As a picture is worth a thousand words we highlight repotting procedures in this way and with these few additional comments your confidence will be sky-high!

The majority of plants to be treated are generally easy to remove from their pots. Ensure the compost is moderately moist. First cut away any roots attached to the outside of the pots. Then spread the fingers of one hand through and between the plant's growths to prevent its fall when you next turn it upside down, give the pot rim a knock on the top side of a bench or table to separate it from the plant; more than one knock may be necessary when a plant is well rooted. Much will be revealed!

Rockwool is increasing in popularity due to its more permanent character; it is not accompanied by problems often posed by bark mixtures

If the root-ball remains intact, is encircled by roots, the compost is sound, we have a candidate ideal for potting-on (dropping-on), without any disturbance, into a larger size pot which has space for a further two years' development. Try the plant inside a selected pot to check for the right size.

If the root-ball falls apart, the compost is decomposed, we have a case for a complete repotting, to remove dead roots, shorten broken live ones back to the point of damage, to discard the old compost, to give the plant a fresh start. This may also be an opportunity to remove surplus backbulbs and to divide a plant (see appropriate illustrations).

Repotting of phalaenopsis is necessary when more space for root growth will be beneficial; however the most common need is when the existing compost is decayed, gives way to pressure of a finger

48

The same plant prepared for repotting, ie all old compost and dead roots removed

When completed the phalaenopsis should appear to be sitting on the compost. If buried too deeply rot may set in

Try prepared plants in empty pots to select the ideal size which comfortably accommodates all the roots without overcrowding

Hold the plant in position with one hand leaving the other free to pour in the compost between the roots; a few sharp taps on the potting table will settle it in and no other firming should be necessary

After-care

Where several plants are potted-on or repotted, colonise them according to the treatment they have received as from now onwards they will need different consideration with regard to watering. The new compost when used should be lightly moist to dry, certainly not wet otherwise any cut or damaged roots will be lost to wet-rot. For the same reason, whether potted-on or repotted, watering should be withheld for four or five days. Subsequently ensure the compost is quite dry, the plants lift very lightly, between waterings; in other words keep them on the dry side. Remember too, larger volumes of compost, as yet unoccupied by the roots, will take longer to dry out. After six to eight weeks potted-on plants are treated as normal. Repotted ones may require extended care until there is root growth and in the meantime are helped with light mistings of rain-water two or three times each day.

49

Repotting almost completed; note the compost is firmed with the flat of the fingers for cymbidiums

A successful policy is to have all the orchids in the same compost. Here we have a cymbidium in rockwool which is to be planted into a bark/peat mixture without any disturbance

Odontoglossums, and similar orchids, are best repotted or potted-on when the new growth is several inches high

Select a pot size which allows two seasons' growth, when the space will be fully occupied and the plant again potted-on

Rockwool for Orchids

Increasingly used in place of peat and/or bark composts, rockwool is an inert medium derived from basalt rock and other minerals, melted at 1500°C, to produce a flock obtainable from most nurserymen. There are various types and grades, sold in granules or larger flock pieces, totally absorbent or water repellent. We have found the absorbent rockwool to be the most successful and the majority of plants produced at the Foundation are now grown in this medium. Many phalaenopsis and cymbidiums

The knife position to cut through the rhizome of this cattleya indicates a division of three pseudobulbs on the right-hand side

Phalaenopsis, dendrobiums and others often produce young plantlets (keikis) which will give true reproductions

sold by garden centres and by nurserymen have probably originated from Holland and Denmark where many hundreds of thousands are produced for the pot-plant trade for sale throughout Europe. Many of them are grown in rockwool easily identified by its white, mottled, wool-like appearance.

Compared with peat or bark composts it has advantages worth consideration. One of the drawbacks of the former is the breakdown, as mentioned earlier, necessitating repotting each two years, more often if the bark is not the best quality. Rockwool never deteriorates and the sole reason for potting will be to provide more space for growth. Another advantage concerns watering; unlike the organic medium, where there is usually a risk of watering too frequently, there are few worries with rockwool which is kept wet most of the time. Therefore the grower must think in terms of hydroponic culture under which an orchid will provide water roots. It will require several months for the changeover from peat and bark mixtures.

As rockwool is inert, nutrient has to be added to the water content and this may be the only drawback so far as amateur growers are concerned; however this is not a deterrent. Commercial producers of orchids and growers at the Foundation have the necessary expensive testing equipment, including computerised control to ensure the plants' requirements are sufficient and correct without any damaging build-up of feed chemicals in the rockwool. Control of the pH is also of associated importance. Inexplicably there is always some opposition to change; on the other hand why change if results with orthodox composts are highly successful? The advantages are too good to be left untried.

Rockwool Culture

As your first orchids may be a rockwool plant, most probably originated as a gift from a garden centre, let us consider its needs. If a changeover from peat and bark is to be made, we present a series of illustrations to meet all situations. As with all types of dry compost the use of a simple dust mask to prevent particles being breathed into the lungs is advisable.

Day to day management will be the same as for other orchids, the exceptions being watering and feed. The same will apply for indoor (window-sill) orchids where rockwool provides an extra benefit because of its wetness and the extra humidity it supplies, especially as there may be a lack of it in a home.

Whatever the circumstances keep rockwool plants together to deal with their special water and feed require-ments. If rain-water is reserved for them worries about chemical content at the outset are diminished; however a pH test is advised, when the nutrient has been added to the water, for acidity or alkalinity. Once an initial test has been made with a pH meter, or carried out by an analyser, any adjustments become routine unless the nutrient is changed.

If any difficulty is anticipated about rain-water supplies this may partly be alleviated by mixing it with equal parts of tap-water.

Most plants will need watering each week during the growing season (this may however depend on the weather and situation) and hydroponic nutrient is added for two consecutive waterings followed by the third of water only, a thorough drenching to eliminate any possible build-up of chemicals.

Root growth of a cymbidium grown in rockwool

and replacing the top inch of rockwool will be advisable where there is much greenness (algae growth). When potting-on or making a change from peat/bark mixtures (see illustrations) work in the rockwool very lightly until it is felt to pack then move on. Not at anytime should much pressure be applied. After-care treatment should be similar to that recommended for peat/bark mixtures.

Resurfacing and Repotting

Each year, prior to or at the beginning of a growing season, resurfacing, removing

52

PROPAGATION

Mericlones, divisions, backbulbs and seedlings

True duplicates of special varieties cannot be raised from seed. This may only be achieved through vegetative propagation and it is now possible, through highly skilled meristem tissue cultures to obtain many thousands of '**Mericlones**' of many outstanding orchids. Consequently, for fairly modest prices, many of the world's best varieties are available and grown by amateurs. Your first orchids may well be mericlones as this mass production is used by European exporters, at the present time as pot plants of cymbidiums, odontoglossums and allied orchids. Another popular orchid, phalaenopsis, is generally raised from seed to flower in three to four years.

Division
In time many orchid plants increase sufficiently in size to permit propagation by division which is the easiest and most successful for amateurs. A count of the number of backbulbs supporting new growths is necessary to ensure a plant is acceptable for division when repotted. Depending on kind a division (or piece), will need two or three backbulbs behind a new growth; for example, a plant may be divided into two pieces each consisting of a new growth supported with three or four backbulbs. Or a smaller division of a new growth and one or two bulbs may be separated from the main plant. According to their size and strength such divisions may produce flowers in a year or two.

Backbulbs
Another way to increase stock is by backbulb propagations. Generally a plant needs at least three backbulbs to support its new growth to ensure good progress and flowering. When repotted others in excess are removed as backbulb propagations or are discarded. An orchid should not be burdened by too many generally leafless backbulbs. The size and number taken will determine the time to flowering, depending on kind, often within a couple of years. If the bulbs are of exceptional size a single backbulb of cymbidium, for example, may be treated as an individual propagation. See illustrations for examples of propagations which include bulblets and off-shoots.

Seedlings
Raising orchids from seed is probably best left to the nurserymen. Each production may require three to eight years to attain flowering. The majority of seedlings raised by nurserymen are made available to the orchid growing public, offered as a single bulb and growth size up to near flowering, priced according to their size and flower potential. They present a marvellous opportunity to share in the raisers' investment offering the possibility of obtaining an orchid of outstanding merit. Until they flower nobody knows! Seedlings usually have exceptional vigour compared to old plants and should be among your first orchids.

HEALTH CARE

Pests: slugs, woodlice, mealy bugs, red spider mites, scale; Diseases: flower spotting, bacterial rot, pseudobulb rot, shrivelling; leaf fall, viruses, non-flowering plants

Fewer pests and diseases attack orchids than other plants; the tough nature of most orchids discourages them. Problems are also minimised by the need for regular and frequent handling to

53

ascertain water requirements and anything unusual is noticed and dealt with before it becomes a serious threat. More often than not troubles are introduced into a collection via new acquisitions and every plant, regardless of its source, should be given a thorough examination for pests or diseases; these must be dealt with before placing them in the company of other plants.

Pests

With your first orchids, or in a small collection of them, pest invasions are so infrequent that routine preventative measures using pesticides are unnecessary. What is needed is conscientious attention to general hygiene; avoid dropping or leaving decaying leaves etc, or any rubbish in the greenhouse. Set aside a large empty flower pot as a

Unusual and different for an intermediate house in *Encyclia brassavolae*, a compact growing species first discovered on the volcano of Chirique in 1848!

Bulbophyllum echinolabium is a species orchid, typical of many from all parts of the world, with unusual and unique flower shape

rubbish bin and empty it often, then hide-outs for the most damaging pests, slugs, snails and woodlice are eliminated. This should equally apply to the outside greenhouse surrounds, particularly with regards to weeds, likely hosts to pests which may find their way inside.

Slugs and snails are the most damaging; they have an uncanny ability of seeking the most highly prized flower spikes to go right through them! Roots and young leaves are often on the menu with phalaenopsis being among their favourite orchids and when these pests nibble holes in small immature leaves, as they gain in growth the holes do too! Pellets of metaldehyde or methiocarb, a dozen or so per square metre of floor space, will deal with these pests, or even more satisfactory after dark when checking all is well, a hand torch soon picks out their slimey trails to lead to the pest.

Woodlice, commonly known 1 cm long greyish pests can at times be troublesome entering plant pots through the drainage holes to breakdown the compost and eat the roots. These are best destroyed as seen by squashing or by seeking out their hideouts (under benches, in empty pots, rubbish, etc) and dusting with an ant powder.

Mealy bugs, easily seen with their whitish mealy coatings, inhabit any plant parts, even flower spikes, if given any freedom to indulge in sap sucking. These are effectively dealt with as seen by dabbing them with an artist's paintbrush loaded with methylated spirit.

Red spider and false spider mites are the most difficult pests likely to be encountered, the former just visible and the latter are invisible to the naked eye. Their presence becomes known, when they are well established, by a silvering of the under surfaces of foliage. The colours of these minute sap-sucking pests is variable according to their ages, from pale almost transparent yellow to a reddish colour. In spite of their small size they can be difficult to eradicate; they obtain a resistance to repeatedly used pesticides. Sprays containing dimethoate, derris, or dicofol used each two or three weeks are usually effective if the spray is concentrated on the undersurfaces of the leaves. When small numbers of plants are concerned the most efficient method is immersion of the whole plant into a bucket of the solution; there is no cause for worry if some enters the compost. Complete coverage is guaranteed. Another successful way of dealing with these mites is to wipe all parts with wetted cotton wool or tissue paper; wipe off cleanly, not working to and from which will only assist in spreading the pest.

Scale insects, although quite small, 3-5 mm, these are readily identified by their shellfish-like shape and hard scale covering over a sap sucking insect. There are two or three kinds, a brown variety being the most common, usually detected by a black sooty mould which develops on a honeydew excretion of the pests. Its destruction is not difficult and depends on efficient removal of the scale insects which tend to hide under rhizomes, leaf bracts and pseudobulb coverings which are best removed. Once again a small artist's bristle brush dipped in methylated spirit is used to gently shift the pest without damage to the plant tissue. Repeat the treatment within a couple of weeks as some are usually missed. If several plants are infected an immersion in a malathion or dimethoate (systemic) solution is preferred to spraying.

Because of the generally robust nature of orchids most pesticides are used on them with safety providing manufacturers' recommended dilutions are

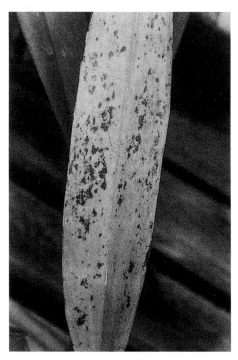

Red spider mites presence is indicated by a silvering of the foliage caused by a multitude of the pest bites

Of the several kinds of scale insect pests the small brown scale is the most common on orchids

closely followed. All precautions for personal safety should be rigidly adhered to, especially a breathing mask used as the likes of malathion or dimethoate are most unpleasant in smell.

Diseases

These are generally the result of a mis-interpretation of plant requirements and mismanagement. The exception is virus diseases to be dealt with later. Each kind of rot or spotting has an identity; how-ever as the cause and treatment of them are similar we will consider only the main

fungal and bacterial rots commonly infecting orchids.

Flower spotting is probably the most common caused by a moisture-laden atmosphere, usually when temperatures are at their lowest at night. Prevention is necessary since spotting is incurable and can only be achieved by restricting damp-down especially in anticipation of lower than ideal temperatures. It often occurs in the spring and autumn when there is little call for artificial heat. Phalaenopsis are particularly prone to flower spotting.

Overmoist, cooler than normal conditions often invite flower spotting botrytis. If possible increase air movement and reduce damping-down

Aphids (greenflies) tend to attack flower buds and young new growths, their presence indicated with a sticky secretion

Bacterial rot may damage any part of a plant. Black or brown areas of wet decay will develop at an alarming pace on pseudobulbs (particularly at the bases), any part which is knocked or bruised, and most susceptible are young growths or matured leaves (as in phalaenopsis), where water has gathered and remains unnoticed for some time. It is important to trace the cause to eventually eliminate the troubles then, as experience is gained, they will diminish and become rare. First check if water is dripping from the greenhouse roof.

Ensure overhead sprayings are light, never heavy to cause a run off into growths. If when watering some falls into leaf centres (phalaenopsis), or in new growths, tip the plants to dislodge the water; (odontoglossums are typical of several kinds likely to be affected).

When rot has set in the decaying part should be removed with a sharp knife or razor blade cutting back to disease-free tissue. In some cases the whole new growth may have to be removed as usually the centre, the growing shoot, has collapsed. Do not despair! These plants are often resurrected by new growth buds from the rhizome. Dust cut surfaces with a sulphur powder or captan, or treat with a bacteriacide such as Physan.

57

Pseudobulb rot is the most worrying when the oldest backbulb turns soft and brown. Considered an ageing factor, it is not generally realised the cause is rot disease within the rhizome (which joins all pseudobulbs). When affected backbulbs are removed by cutting through the rhizome. Ensure the cut is clean; if there is a brown centre present, the disease remains in the rhizome. To completely eliminate this rot a cut must be made back to clean disease-free tissue, even if it involves removal of an apparently healthy pseudobulb. Treat the cut surface of the rhizome as described for bacterial rot.

Shrivelling pseudobulb may be of concern to newcomers. Generally it is due to the enormous demands on a plant's reserves to bear flowers. In many orchids, if a comparison is made, it will be discovered the amount of spike and flower material exceeds the size of the pseudobulb it comes from and is bound to cause stress. It is a natural condition and no reason for worry. The exception will be if shrivelling is accompanied by yellowing of the foliage which indicates loss of roots.

Leaf fall. Understandably a newcomer to orchid growing becomes anxious at signs of leaves beginning to yellow. There may be the occasion when such anxiety is justified but generally it is part of an ageing process; it may occur at anytime of the year but is more pronounced during autumn and winter. Allow such leaves to yellow, ripen and fall naturally. The time to be concerned is when several leaves of different ages, particularly the younger ones, yellow at the same time. Sadly the problem then goes deeper, concerns the roots, the loss of them and demise of many plants. The condition is generally the result of too-frequent waterings confirmed by exam-

Shows a cymbidium with symptoms of mosaic virus which, in this case, does not appear to affect the vigour of the plant

ining the rootball; the dead roots will be brown and soft. If on the otherhand the roots are white and sound there is good cheer as prolonged dryness is corrected firstly by immersing the rootball into water for a short time, until air bubbles cease rising and then follow with more frequent waterings than previously. Aided by stored reserves of the pseudobulb, or thick fleshy leaves, recovery of plants suffering from root loss is reasonably assured by immediate repotting, increased warmth and keeping the new compost on the dry side until new roots are produced.

Virus diseases. There are several kinds of viruses which affect the leaves and flowers of orchids (see illustration,

58

In severe cases the flowers are affected by the virus. Such plants are best destroyed

One method of control when cutting any parts is to utilise cheap double-sided razor blades which are discarded after use. Another is to sterilise cutting tools using a 10% solution of household bleach; treatment should be for at least ten seconds and the bleach solution should be changed once it has lost its distinctive smell.

It will be unfair to give virused plants or propagations to others.

Non-flowering plants. Without doubt the most perplexing and common problem. If we could see the plants and the conditions under which they are grown we could, nine times out of ten, offer a solution. The difficulty is there are so many reasons why a plant does not flower. Most complaints are about cymbidiums (see 'Where to grow them', page 29); usually it is due to the plants having insufficient time to make strong enough growth. No doubt your first orchid was taken into the home, without any knowledge of its need, kept there for several weeks until the flowers died. The plant has to recover, renew growth, probably without the aid of a greenhouse. For at least a year expectations have to be low for such beginnings.

First and foremost must be sufficient size and strength according to the kind of orchid; if there has been some deterioration the odds for flowering are much reduced. An early start of new growth in the spring is essential and dependent on adequate warmth; it will be delayed if minimum temperatures are the norm. A few degrees of extra warmth at this time will motivate plants into early root action and growth with the advantages of a longer season and in the end larger matured growth for flower production. A difference of at least 5°F between night and day temperatures is required at all times and towards the end

page 58). In some cases the plant will deteriorate in size and strength; in others they will continue to maintain growth and flower production year after year and the owners are unlikely to respond to advice about destroying the plants. A further difficulty is some orchids do not reveal the presence of virus unless stressed in some way or other.

The orchid collection is yours and your responsibility. If you retain virus-infected plants be aware the disease is mainly spread when cutting tools are used, when the sap of a virused plant is transferred to the sap of a healthy one. Viruses are not often spread by mere contact. Unfortunately there is not any known cure.

of the growth season it is vital for flower initiation.

Another reason for failure to bloom is insufficient light to produce good firm leaves and pseudobulbs. In a mixed house of orchids it may be difficult to provide the ideal for each kind; however when a well-grown plant refuses to flower move it to another position with more light or slight change of temperature. Such treatment requires patience; non-flowering plants need the benefit of a whole growing season to respond, not a few weeks in different positions. Eventually as your enthusiasm and the size of your collection grows, overcrowding may inhibit flowering of some kinds; each plant needs its share of good light.

The ambition and purpose of every plant is to reproduce through flowering and seeds; often when an orchid is undersized, in desperation it will attempt flowering. In such cases give preference to health and strength by nipping out the flower spike at an early stage; it will repay with larger growths.

Finally what the plants tell us makes all the difference between success and failure. Plants with lush, dark green, soft, floppy growths are suffering from insufficient light and are reluctant to bear flower spikes. With intense light growth will be bleached of its green colour; brown areas of burn may appear. Ideally orchid plant growth should be firm, upstanding and a light olive-green colour.

Cattleyas, considered the more glamorous orchids, are also among the
easiest to grow and flower, particularly species *Cattleya labiata*

PART THREE

POPULAR FIRST ORCHIDS

Cymbidiums, Paphiopedilums, Miltonias, Odontoglossums and Odontiodas and Phalaenopsis

Cymbidiums originate from the foothills of the Himalayas stretching into Thailand and China, and are the most easily obtainable orchid as a pot plant. According to many growing manuals it is 'the easiest of all orchids to grow'. We think this is an inaccurate statement; it should read 'the most difficult orchid to kill'.

The reason for the cymbidiums' popularity is probably the long life of the flowers, anywhere between six and twelve weeks. The flowering season lasts from October through to May, achieved by using different species in the hybridising. Size varies enormously with some plants in 12 inch pots with foliage reaching three feet high, only suitable for decorating the hall. The most popular type in this genus is the so-called 'mini-cymbidium'. These are the result of breeding a very small species onto a large type, creating a flowering plant in a six inch pot with foliage just one foot high. Colours are varied; yellow, green, pink and white are the dominant shades.

Cymbidium Goldrun, like most modern varieties, need good light, very little shading when in full growth

Cymbidium Leoville 'Trinity', intermediate in plant size, is considered a miniature. Prolific in flowering these orchids are sold in large numbers in garden centres etc, and may be your first orchid

The fine white with a magnificent lip is *Cymbidium* Portelet Bay 'Trinity' AM/RHS

A smaller version of the standard cymbidium has gained in popularity due to less demands on space. *Cym* Fliquet 'Trinity' is a lovely example

One of the problems encountered with cymbidiums is a shyness to produce flowers. Cymbidiums need a light position with a drop of temperature at night in order to reflower and this is difficult in a house. Success has been achieved by standing cymbidiums out-of-doors in the summer, after any chance of frost, in the south of England, June until late September. They should be kept in a shady position, ideally under an apple tree in dappled shade where plants or grass will grow. Failing this any shady spot will suffice. Vigilence is needed to prevent slugs and snails devastating new flower spikes.

Lycastes such as *Lyc* Amaroo 'St Helier' AM/RHS, are excellent companions for cymbidiums as they enjoy similar conditions

Maxillaria picta, a species from Brazil, produces clusters of single flowers from the bases of its pseudobulbs and prefers cool conditions

Species *Coelogyne cristata* will add variety where cymbidiums dictate the cultural conditions

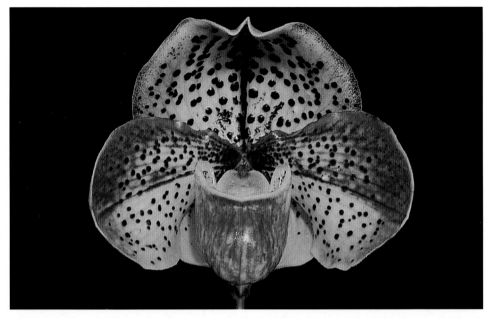

Paphiopedilum es Pigneaux and numerous similar hybrids are splendid subjects for growing in a home, on a window-sill or tea-trolley

Paphiopedilums are commonly known as the 'Ladies Slipper Orchid', due to the unique shape of the flower, a pouch on the front of the bloom. Paphiopedilums make fine pot plants with each flower born on a single stem; they are long lived, sometimes up to ten weeks. Paphiopedilums are terrestrial plants requiring little in the way of feed. In their natural habitat most of the roots travel amongst the leaves and moss on the forest floor. Culturally it is a fine orchid for the living room providing it does not receive direct sun and the compost is kept moist as they do not have a bulb with reserved nutrient like many other orchids. The great majority of this genus flower through the winter months.

Top left: The majority of Slipper Orchid Hybrids owe their origin to this cool growing plain leaved species *Paphiopedilum insigne*

Top right: Another popular easily grown species is *Paphiopedilum argus*, ideal for home growing

Bottom left: Paphiopedilum primulinum is valued for producing a succession of flowers

Bottom right: The larger growing strap-leafed *Paphiopedilum* species and hybrids, such as this superb *Paph* Transvaal, will appreciate generous warmth at all times

66

67

A lovely inexpensive species for the cool house is *Paphiopedilum hirsuttismum*

An arrangement of Slipper Orchids with foliage plants will give pleasure for at least a couple of months

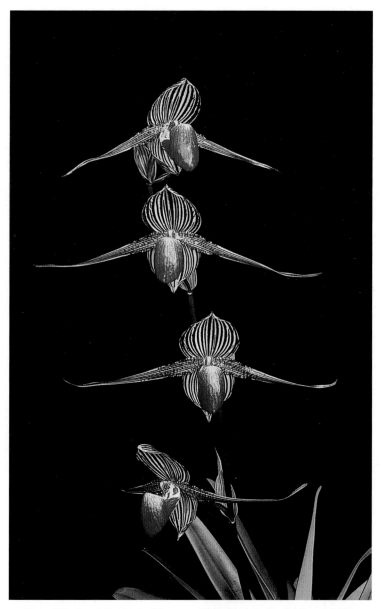

One of the finest *Paphiopedilum* species is *Paph rothschildianum* with flowers 30 cm wide

Odontoglossums and Odontiodas have the common name 'Butterly Orchid'. They require more specific growing conditions as the original species come from the South American mountains. Although of tropical latitude these plant have evolved at high elevations of up to seven thousand feet in the Andes, consequently they need light, cool, growing conditions. With the hybridist inter-crossing this type they have created some magnificent varieties that are grown as pot plants. They flower mostly in spring to summer.

Two varieties of *Odontioda* Eric Young 'Rozel' (above) and 'Isle of Jersey' (left), both AM/RHS, show variations within a hybrid

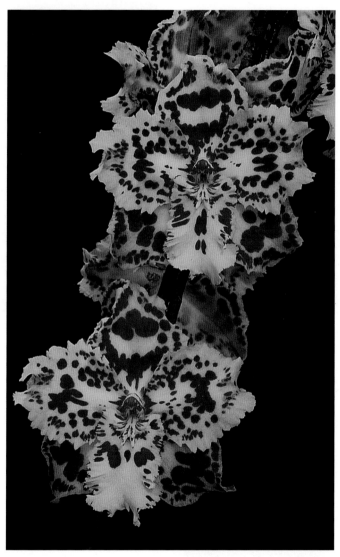

Orchids are extraordinary for their intergeneric breeding and this beautiful *Odontocidium* La Rocque 'St Ouen' AM/RHS originated from an *Odontoglossum* crossed with an *Oncidium*

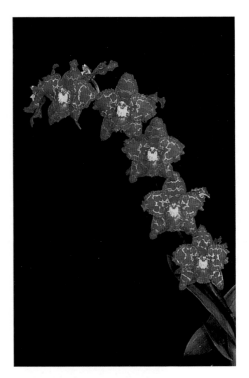

Odontioda West Mount 'Trinity' illustrates the delightful floral designs of orchids which may be grown in a home on window-sills

Top left: Odontioda Portelet Bay is an example of their right bright colours

Many Odontoglossum species are being raised from seed and Odm bictoniense is one often seen in cool house collections

72

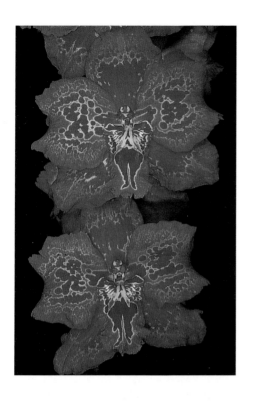

Miltonias originate from Colombia. The common name for this plant is 'Pansy Orchid', aptly named due to the flatness of the flower. This orchid has recently become a major pot plant for indoor culture as the flowers last for up to six weeks. The colours vary from the deepest red through to pink, white and yellow and are often very vibrant in colour. This is a beautiful mainly summer flowering plant.

Odontiodas are noted for their brilliant colours and flower designs such as this fine *Oda* L'Etacq 'Trinity'

Below: This is a fine specimen Pansy Orchid, *Miltoniopsis* Brutips

Phalaenopsis are commonly known as the 'Moth Orchid', receiving this name when they were first seen hanging from the branches of trees with their flowers fluttering in the breeze. They are mostly in the pink to white colour range and variants between. While the natural growing conditions for these plants is hot and humid, with limited light requirements, experience has proved that phalaenopsis are the most accommodating of the tropical orchids used as pot plants in ordinary living room conditions. It is not unusual to see the plants grow and flower happily for a number of years indoors. Being an orchid that grows naturally in a tropical environment all year through, grown indoors these plants will tend to flower almost non-stop; the plant should be allowed to recover after flowering by cutting the finished flower spike off near the base of the plant, thus allowing a new flower stem to emerge. Three to four months are needed for the new flowers to open. Alternatively the old flower stem can be left on the plant and it is possible that a spike will start from a dormant bud, but there is a danger that the plant will become overtaxed.

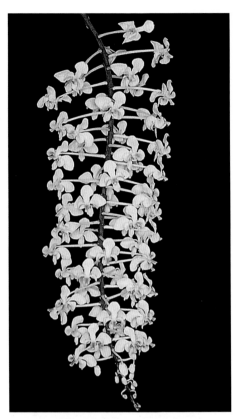

Quite different to the large flowered Moth Orchids is the multiflowered *Phalaenopsis celebensis* 'Trinity' AM/RHS

The individual flowers of *Phalaenopsis violacea* are long lasting

Phalaenopsis interbred with *Doritis* has resulted in rich coloured and heavily lined flowers: *Doritaenopsis* Maufant 'Trinity' is a fine example

Phalaenopsis Corbière, raised at the Foundation, has extra large flowers

A warm section of 65°-70°F which is mostly shaded from bright light, will be dominated by the popular *Phalaenopsis* such as *Phal* Lady Jersey 'Mont Millais'

Left: Yellow flowered *Phalaenopsis* Sierra Gold is a new colour development

Far right: Petal-splashed primary hybrid *Cattleya* Interglossa

Near right: Smaller *Sophrolaeliocattleya* Tiger Rag is ideal for a window-sill

Some of the most illustrious orchid blooms are produced by *Cattleya* and *Laelia* and intergeneric hybrids. *Bc* Mem Helen Brown has 10 cm (4 inches) wide fragrant flowers

Pompadour-type *Dendrobium* Ekapol 'Panda', a tall growing hybrid, is representative of a group of intensely rich colours which will enjoy conditions as for phalaenopsis

Catasetum fimbriatum one of the 'Trigger Orchids' shoots out its pollinia when touched. A long rest is needed after flowering

Part of the Eric Young Orchid Foundation RHS Gold Medal display at the
Chelsea Flower Show, 1991

One of the many orchid vistas in the Display House at the Eric Young Orchid Foundation which is
open to the public on every Wednesday, Thursday, Friday and Saturday

Index to Illustrations

Photographic Credits: Martin Ahring (EYOF)
John Blowers
The Orchid Review